Purple Dark
The Language of Chaos

Purple Dark
Language of Chaos

De'Broada Cornelius

iCreativ Books
Kansas

iCreativ Books
an imprint of iCREATIV PROPERTI, LLC.
6505 E. Central Suite #314
Wichita KS 67206

Purple Dark: Language of Chaos
Copyright © 2017 by, De'Broada L. Cornelius

iCreativ Books supports copyright. Copyright fuels creativity, encourages diverse voices and promotes free speech. iCreativ Books has allowed this work to remain exactly as the author intended, verbatim, without editorial input.

All rights reserved including the right to reproduce this book or portions thereof in any form whatsoever. For information address iCreativ Properti, LLC, to obtain written permission of the publisher, 6505 E. Central Suite #314, Wichita KS 67206

Printed in the United States of America.

Purple Dark: Language of Chaos.
ISBN: 978-0-692-95285-6

iCreativ Books
6505 E. Central Suite #314,
Wichita KS 67206
www.icreativproperti.com

For, people who want to read what I have to say.

CONTENTS
Chasm

Chasm (Chaos)	2
Poetreé Call	3
Write Right Now	4
Purple Dark	5
Langue' Chaotic	7
Seeds	8
Flexing	9
Sigh	9
Locked Up	10
Tension	12
Progress	13
Constant Fuel	14
Rebel's Prayer	15
Shadows	17
Don't Know	19
WTH	20
Absent Mind	22
Threads	23
Breakthrough	25
Snapback	25
Assignment	26
Fear Not	27
This Morning	28
Oneness	29
B You	30

Trenches

Trenches	34
Don't Wanna	35
So Good	36
Sorting	37
Pity Pot	38
Heart	39
Pieces of Me	39
Shadow-talk	40
Stuck	41
Masquerade	42
Hangovers	43
Calloused	44
Potholes & Pits	45
Down	46
Hatred's Prayer	47
Girl Whirl	50
Wildflower	51
Sometimes	52
I Let Him	54
Logic	58
Bad Fruit	59
Serendipity	61
Junkie Mind	63
Can't	64
Choices	65
Petty	66
Aware	66
Quitting Time	67
Who This?	68
Bargaining	70
Missing You	72

Good Grief	74
Personal	75
Too Much Sauce	77
I Emot	79
Blame	80

Isness

Isness	83
My Day	84
Coffee	84
Composition	85
Indecision	86
Dirty	87
U Stop U	89
Matchup	90
Interview	91
Let Go	93
Go Just Go	94
Me Time	95
Super Hero	98
Hush	99
Blockhead	101
Moved	102
LOL	104
Other Side	105
Hang Up	107
Self-Trap	108
Selfish	109
Warnings	110
Self-Seduction	111
Sometimes II	114
Changed	116
Fleeting II	117

Thought	117
Yum Yum	118
First Thing	119
Sweet Spot	121
IDK	121
Walls	122
Mistakes	123
Truth Juice	125
Speak-easy	126
Kinsman	126
Read Me	127
Proposals	128
Blackberry Kisses	129
Ummm	130
Ummm 2	131
No Benies	132
aRt	133
Just Saying	133
Thank You	134
Do	136
About the Author	137

v

Chasm (Chaos)

In the silence, there is true. I'm doing something with my potential. How about you?

De'Broada

Chasm (Chaos)

Patience and love I demand while bringing words of my true. For I live with the chaos inside so, I must speak of it to you. Nothing is ever ok and everything is always alright. I can capture you with words and can take you anywhere. The best thing about it, is you wouldn't care... for the moment. Because the moment is what we live for. To be transported moved, turned on, tuned in to the narrative of our own life. For we can't leave our self alone.

My voice matches the consciousness within exposing sin... allowing you to see, the perfect collective mess called "me." For, this is who I am and what you think you need me to be, for survival of your distorted fantasy. Therefore, fit me into the box you made and I'll project light on your mind shade... to help you see me better. Sometimes a mess just needs to be confessed placing demons in a state of rest. Friend of mine are you doing your best or, worried about the rest?

Poetreé Call

I have I have poetry poetreé

Who harkens to hear creativity?

Energy of words

Gift chosen me

I have I have poetry poetreé

Expression of emotion my delight

Feeding on words obvious and trite

Distinguish truth's intensity

Rhythms of language create melody

Word diet—false, hopeless, absurd

Closed eyes see all that's heard

Conditions the burden of mortality

Impaired view creates reality

I have I have poetreé for you my friend

Taking your thoughts

beyond where they have been

Write Now

All I can do right now is

Write

This moment, this time

Stay connected with One mind

Write unite with insight

Dreamt of blue light

From body to the sky

Contrite heart cannot lie

Stay ahead of the whistle

Signal call of the dead

A promised dwelling place

Are the words in my head?

Offer no excuses or shifts no blame

A modified heart carries its shame

For blessed are those who mourn

So, I write

Purple Dark

Belly tense with anger

Sour sadness, desperation, danger

Is this madness?

What lesson has this feeling?

Awareness quiet rage

Enemy's path to healing

Collect not, forget not, old tears of pain

Stored sorrow makes the heart of face change

Oh, to be free of life's vexation

Running game on yourself changes vibration

Scream, shout, let it out

Still, be still near the frequency of doubt

Chase not, erase not, why live out a lie

A point of self-hatred and want to die

Joy's high is gone snuffed out is light

Universe move swiftly this shit ain't right

Not taking care of self

Doing what I don't want to do

Words attack personality

It's you against you

Master of mind changes over time

To thine own-self be true

Use the mirror of accountability

See the jerk in view

Detach from the "actor"

Remember who are you

The edge of outer is not very far

Self-hatred a dark purple path

You must decide to save your own ass

Langue Chaotic (language of chaos)

It's not the devastation of lies that surprise

It's the pride in eyes which you cannot hide

Pushing out your lips pretending not to hear

Truth being heard by your attentive ear

The denial of love ones flippin' off appeal

Eating at your soul tattooed with a seal

Seal of destruction weakened connectivity

Pretend all you want, I know you hear me

It's not the construction of lies or, betrayal of trust

Arrogant pride is the real disgust

No one owes you anything

Truth you refuse to see

Screw up your life affects you not me

There's not a problem understanding you

Pain is universal this isn't new

No judge of situation not after you friend

Pray emotional distress lead to divinity within

I trusted you

Seeds

Seeds planted deep in mind

Worry 'bout race, progress, time

Things I can't change

Running to and from pain

Work

Taught to hustle, pray things go my way

Things I can't control

So much I want to say

Do

Make moves, take risks, win, lose

Slow pace, sit in faith

Ponder over which path to take

Looking for the Great Escape!

Game of Thrones

Dorothy said there's no place like home

As I roam... all alone

Trying to figure this sh** out

Flexing

Flexing...mood is rude

Thought is naught

What do you want?

Sigh...

Tired of feeling like nobody

Know what I mean?

Tired of feeling like nobody

While someone else is living my dream

Is that lie true?

I'm who's fascinating

I haven't reached my height

Habit of hesitating

Keeps affecting my flight

Lord help me

Locked UP

Got that locked up feeling

I'm irritated

Got that locked up feeling

Is my mind reprobated?

Idolized thought indoctrinated

Filled with frustration

I've looked everywhere

Can't find one soul that seem to care

Forgetting again to look within

There I'll find my truest friend

Got that locked up feeling

He's not around

She won't answer the phone

He's making noise

I'm left all alone

Stay in shower hours at a time

Drowning the mind with red wine

Am I in labor?

Am I birthing me?

Eyes wide open

Mountain of Elephant's I see

Got that locked up feeling

Somethings got to give

Release me from me so I can live

Tension

Outer edge of distance's view

Profound period of tension 2

Feel deprived of something that's mine

Prayer opens portals seek the divine

Days unending when under attack

Why can't I hear you...do you have my back?

Can't validate, relate to who I am

Beyond alone and don't give a damn

Locked in a flower bed of emotion

Anger my new friend has my devotion

Tender hearted father promises I can't see

Recognize my suffering I'm blind spiritually

Motives of my motive are fear based

Anger's perception I've began to embrace

Sour sadness, desperation, danger

Say the savior of soul was born in a manger

Progress

Undermining of progress stress could achieve

In and out of life continue to weave

Longing for conditions that equal ease

Custom made adversity guaranteed

Who made it to heaven?

Who ate the bread?

Unity unleavened

Is the master dead?

Cast a net of opportunity

Ego blocks receptivity

Undermining stress progress could achieve

Know how to survive but not to succeed

Shifted mind state there's a great unknown

Trust the light of truth

It will lead you home

Constant Fuel

Feel anger more than before

Sedated with euphemisms not anymore

Substituted darkness with self-talk

Lead down a road called "My Walk"

Guilt pit-stop to humble threshold

Wayward thoughts don't increase the load

Keep up keep moving let the path unfold

Don't arrest thoughts like I use to

Eons of experience guide me through

Don't look for big picture...the fullness of scope

The quest for seeing, hearing...the intensity of hope

Not anymore

Magnetize your energy field

Anger is fuel

Use it to heal

Rebel's Prayer

You just don't do me right

I ask for more and...

All I get is the bread of life?

I want things...lover of my dreams

Cars, money, houses

All the stuff I see

Eyes crave man-made prosperity

Live outside my means

Wanna be part of the scene

Hooked like a fiend on symbols and things

Keep up with the Jones'—status dreams

Increase debt and beg for more

Possess everything...still feel poor

Looking for the come up and the free meal

Want food that perishes not food that heals

The food you give won't fulfill lust

So, I say that just ain't enough

Discontent filled... too foolish to repent

Never give a tenth of one cent

Amplified vibration from my soul I take
Once again, a foolish mistake
The bread of life...heard about it
Some say can't live without it
Yahweh sounds like yo' way to me
Blasphemy speaks a fool can't see
Radically heal my iniquity
Show me the speed of suddenly
Satisfy hunger quench my thirst
Shift my vibration ignite my trust
7 times "I am" the truth and light
Please share your cup
Before my day turns to night
I need the bread of life

Shadows

Alone on my own antagonist stand

Taking steps unknown in snow or sand

Grace of God or destiny's plan

Here I am

In mind, hear the shadow speak

Bearing truth believe in defeat

No place safe for me to retreat

Here I am

Faith, father, friend hard to conceive

Lost hope in love too empty to perceive

Rather eat a bullet than risk and believe

Here I am

This is halfway I can't travel no more

No running from my fate

Let's settle the score

Shadow of despair whipped me to and fro'

Broken spirit...Here I am

Power over circumstance

Trembling with ease

Relate and release decide what you believe

The Rabbit Hole does not care

It will take the mind anywhere

Antagonistic adversary shadow I see

Fatalism is ego's prophecy

Don't Know

Don't know what to do

Don't know who to become

Words loaded

Like a "effing" gun

I turn on myself

Try to describe

The way dying feels

Deep inside, I want to live

Watching time no one hears

Choose to overcome

Or, be ruled by fears

WTH

Why live or, even give a damn?

Why give or, even live a damn?

Can you follow me?

The who I am, not the who you see

Sustained by mercy taking up space

Molding mind accepting grace

Mental labor of circumstance

Experience oneness delicate dance

For him if given a chance

I'd do it again

Correct the err of sin

With love

Sacrifice, suffer for another's well being

A stage of the journey where eyes start seeing

Look out...doubt will come... will pass

Love in heart will endure outlast

Why search for blame?

A mother's stamp bears no shame

Who do you hate? Invalidate?

The man of poor faith
Who's taken so long to awake
Glorified excuses filled with pride
Ego pleasures changing wives and lives
Unaware of the practice of self-defeat
Wobbling between absence and retreat
Truth is...
Most people want what they are not
There is no mystery you get what you put out

Absent Mind

Who never knows what's going on?

The liar denier

Witness knows this doesn't exist

Truth knows what lies to resist

Making the choice of not to partake

World of seed he chose to co-create

The work at hand requires a lifetime

Fragmented effort eats the heart of the mind

Disrespects the plan of Divine

Perfects the condition of absent mind

Wrapped in self, knowledge becomes very clear

You can't teach if you're not here

Placing perfectly your love out of reach

Presence is required for you I cannot speak

Mommy, where is my daddy?

Threads

Trauma does last always

Things do fall apart

Don't know where you're heading

Understand the perception of thought

On a surface to be sold

Some stories are never told

Mystery history never free

Man craves captivity

Ethnic cleansing is genocide

Break wind is still pass gas

Between jobs is unemployed

Arithmetic is still math

Parallel realities seem simple

Until you expose the rest

I saw the sea of forgiveness

Away it took my breath

Equipped to cope

Forced into conditions

Changed vantage point

To clearly see position

Escalated degree of discomfort

Connected mind to space

Couldn't define knew the sound

Had to embrace

Trauma does last always

Things do fall apart

Attachment to self is darkness

When trapped inside your heart

Follow the threads

Breakthrough

I can hear the voice of others

not my own

I talk to myself and call it breakthrough

And I laugh heartily at you

Snapback

Maybe death could snap

you out of your dream

then perhaps

you'll understand

what life means

Assignment

Remember what is true

Follow the narrow road make it thru

Save the heroics

Lies you can't undo

Wake from mad things

killing you

Nothing is as it seems

Giant shadows, strong drink, strange places

Find a space among alien faces

Assignment of blindness

Has been given you

Follow the narrow road make it thru

Fear Not

I am one

Infinite power lives within

Overcome your condition

Let the games begin

The right time is now

Create what you want

No perfect moment awaits

Either you do or don't

There's nothing to fear

Come from under your spell

Your time will expire

And you'll regret like hell

This Morning

All this thought processing

Ain't trying to 'splain

Stress or consciousness

Thoughts rest on the negative

Where do you live?

This morning I took a positive pill

Oneness

Didn't wake up on the outside of me

Didn't saturate my brain with internet or tv

Moved not in direction of the illusions I see

Experienced clarity and harmony

Didn't wake in opposition

No battle in mind

No turmoil or indecisiveness

No situation to define

No complaining just remaining

No breech of self love

Just the Oneness of oneness

And grace from above

Today is a good day

B You

You can never be what you are not.

You can only give what you got.

A bed is not a cot.

You must run not trot.

to Zion

What's cold is not hot.

Expect to get what you got.

'Cause you asked for it

Trouble comes your way

A set number of days

Alchemist optimist

Can't increase the sun's rays

We pay a price for living in the sky

Close your eyes and don't ask why

These are lessons of this degree

Seek spheres of higher activity

Acquire wealth don't be ashamed

Practice release don't store pain

Do your work faithfully

For in the forest fell a tree

Maintain a level of sobriety

Never get sick off of luxury

Always assess your energy

Be inspired

Trenches

Down in the dirt you gotta do the work.

Trenches

Consistently filled with disgruntlement.

This life can't be what the good lord meant.

Bitch, moan, complain all day

Turbulent mind in full play

Adopted European appetite for greed

Thinking distorted ego feeds

Conflicting desires want feel like need

A castle of trenches I've entered indeed

Don't Wanna

Don't wanna ain't gonna

I don't give a damn what is said

No one likes to do the thing they dread

From going to work to making the bed

No one likes to do the thing they dread

Life doesn't require cooperation from you

Get uncomfortable

I hate to do

Desire for ease and comfort pursue

Dead is sacrifice and chivalry too

I don't give a damn what is said

No one likes to do the thing they dread

I'm here for me not for you

Don't wanna, ain't gonna

What's your true?

So Good

You've gotten so good

Never letting go

Monsters chase the mind

Your sh** just grow

Don't ask a damn thing

I told you so

Waiting for the next time

to say "I don't know?"

Sorting

Sorting through contention

Won't acknowledge or mention

It took three hours to move out of my way

On what side of the pain is delay

Are you judging these words

before you read through?

Tell me, tell me who are you?

Don't be the dummy on your lap

Wrapped in strings of limitation

A calcified mind filled with doubt

Breeds trepidation

I capture thoughts freeze them on paper

To help you understand your situation

You drain me

Pity Pot

Everyday wake hoping not

Take a seat on the pity pot

Waiting to see... waiting to be

Something more than who you see

Loyal companion day and night

Never see anything else in sight

Waiting for you as you sleep

Self-pity wallowing sentimentality

Enemy of happiness called anxiety

Competes with clarity creates a mess

Carpet your feet along the stroll of stress

Get up, do the work own your life

Carrying burdens is your strife

Decide to change your situation

Where you end is a chosen destination

Figure it out on the way down

Pity pot sitting room for clowns

And that's that

Heart

Heart must match energy

There is no short cut

Where you hold your mind

Is where you'll find your rut

Pieces of Me

Soft parts are becoming hard

I always wondered

How mama got like that

Life will reach and teach

God is not Santa Claus

Love and hate

Can cause you to pause

Power is a cycle

Hot eyes waging war

What chu' lookin' at me for?

Shadowtalk

Want me to trust you?

I can't, better yet I won't

I don't

You're like the eagle in the sky

A breeze from the depth of ocean passing by

Blazing sun of summer

Morning star of East,

Unity of God's wildebeest

Beautifully profound as one can see,

Cleverly disguised—you're the enemy

Get thee behind me!

Stuck

In what appears to be a rut

Covered flesh created from dirt

Sometimes eyes hurt

Release pain—cut

Others with my tongue

Sometimes it's fun

Mind is the loaded gun

Tying to look back while you run

Stuck

In what appears to be a rut

Sometimes eyes hurt

Avoid pain—lie

Don't allow self to cry

Love's a sweet lullaby

Masquerade

You're not alright with you

Observer of what you do

You see what you keep putting yourself through

Masquerade you're not alright with you

Martyrdom continue to choose

Justifying situations where you lose

Walk, talk, act confused

Allow ego to coerce you

You're not alright with you

You know what you keep putting yourself through

Keenly aware every step you take

Running game on yourself reality you make

Refusing to choose to sever the ties

Masquerade another word for disguise

Hangovers

Life of a liar is hard to maintain

Tormenting the mind is a fool's game

O, the effort required performing the sneak

Hangover from conscious makes the spirit weak

Sharing secrets with the heart

Gambling with one's soul

Ageing from the inside where truth unfolds

Evil watches she's the wife of death

As the grave prepares for its next theft

O, the life of a liar hard to maintain

A fool always loses at a fool's game

Calloused

Burned…infection of rejection

Poisoned plague of desire

Running doesn't change truth

When dealing with a liar

Without hope can you cope?

Accept your place on this plain

Not knowing you're the joke

Illusions choke life out of sane

What do you do when true isn't true?

Please answer me…I'm talking to you

Rejection's pathway has triggers

What's ignored grows bigger

Things don't just happen is in all the teachings

Is this karmic life which I'm speaking?

Potholes n' Pits

Potholes n' pits

Where you sit and cry

Nursing pools of why o' why

Wondering plundering

Can hope die?

Yes, if you let it

Living under the sun don't wanna return

Forgive let go of what's been done

Do we really connect with old love ones?

Why want what doesn't feel good to you?

How'd you get turned from chasing true?

What exactly are you running to?

Burden shoes always walk in shame

Potholes n' pits are filled with pain

Where are you walking?

Down

Broke me down

Didn't hang around

Feel like a clown

Rain pours down

Fury

Tried to destroy

Don't know what was the ploy

Something about hurting

Gave him joy

But I hope he dies early

No reason to be so cruel

Now I use hate as a tool

Language broken left behind

Up is down in your mind

Hatred's Prayer

Saw someone I hate

It wasn't a mistake

Walked up shook my hand

Holy, holy, holy almighty God

Who, was and is to come

With what do I do with my hate

Thy will must be done

Must thy will be done?

Holy, holy, holy almighty God

Power I must access

Black-hearted evil from head to toe

Bless him with unrest

Be a weight upon his shoulders

From which he cannot lift his head

Holy, holy, holy almighty God

I really wish he was dead

Turn to you what shall I do

In you there is no defect

Correct the deficiency in me

For I cannot detect

Satisfy lust for justice and revenge

A righteous strike to his days begin

Place his head on a platter

Emotional turmoil his lot

Evilness of his ways

Earned him an early plot

Thief of dreams

There's nothing's clean

Regrettable acts he performed

Many threatened and harmed

The facts aren't distorted

Restitution don't prolong

There must be responsibility

For his doing wrong

Please, please, oh, please I beg

Give him infinite despair

For consequence is the reason

Leave him all alone

Let storms be his constant season

Decrease his understanding

Increase his participation

Make heavy his guilty conscious

Hell, his final destination

He stole inner innocence

Led many astray

Introduced darkness

Into a blessed day

Bedded kindred flowers

Left them all alone

Guaranteed hatred of self

Created a mental war zone

May burden wrap his head like a turban

Illuminate his path with pain

Let self-disgust be his mantra

From the good book wipe his name

Amen

Girl Whirl

Why do I look and think I'm not beautiful?

Words cannot explain

I see myself in the mirror

Comments I hear are deranged

Rearranged coming from inside

Psychological theories of beauty loaded

From which I cannot hide

Referencing difference taunting my unique

Criticizing self, dreadful cycles of repeat

For sick reason, I believe I'm not

Continue to cover all that I've got

Beauty land girl whirl of druthers

Rite of passage learn from mothers

You must see the view of the treasure

True beauty has no physical measure

So, why do I look and think...?

Wildflower

Just because he misused you

Doesn't make you useless...beauty

Some try to kill what lives

Because they're already dead

Beautiful wildflower placed in his hands

Seeking protection sin eats the heart of man

You must understand the true violation

Before you can change the situation

Fragmented innocence worthy enough

Hold on to the truth present at birth

Don't look at yourself through others eyes

Fiction is another word for lies

You are worthy

Sometimes

Sometimes I can't tell

My demons from my angels

Both appear during hard times

Desiring to takeover life

Language sounds like noise

Do I chase the divine?

Or hit another line

Both will end up in rhyme

Passion is never surprised by attack

Can you tell me where Jesus at?

Fever of comparison killing me

Fear is suppressed insecurity

I don't know why moma left

I'm told life is a gift

More than pure gold

My mental can't avoid the rift

Exception to the rule

Experience of strife

Demons from my angels

A school called life

Sometimes I can't tell

My demons from my angels

Both appear during hard times

Leading to many doorways of the mind

I Let Him

He beats me he doesn't complete me

He beats me he doesn't complete me

He beats me he doesn't complete me

And I let him

Today I'm glad to be alive

But from him I cannot hide

To leave him I've tried

Last night I dreamt I'd died

He beats me he doesn't complete me

He beats me he doesn't complete me

He beats me he doesn't complete me

And I let him

Him I wish I didn't know

Into this how did we grow

Is this how you show—love?

His Daddy did and so did brother

I'm addicted to him like no other

Every book has its cover

And I let him

He beats me he doesn't complete me

He beats me he doesn't complete me

He beats me he doesn't complete me

And I let him

Doesn't choke me anymore

Just shoves my face against the floor

Calls me names like bitch and whore

And I let him

I don't know how to stop

Playing roulette with my life

Says he wants me to be his wife

That's when I pick up the knife

And...cut my wrist

To avoid his fist

No longer do I want to exist

In this pain

Love's torrential rain

Look at how much weight I've gained

My family is angry and ashamed

Cause I let him

He beats me he doesn't complete me
He beats me he doesn't complete me
He beats me he doesn't complete me
And I let him
I've learned to live inside fear
My own voice I no longer hear
He makes his words sound so sincere
When he says "I'm sorry"
No one understands him like I do
When he's violent he doesn't mean too
It only happens when he's drinking
This might sound like wishful thinking
Please don't think I've never fought
Threw away the things he's bought
It's just that I'm caught
In a cycle of death
He beats me he doesn't complete me
He beats me he doesn't complete me
And I let him

It takes more than courage
To walk away from this life
Does love exist without abuse and strife
And god?
I've packed my things several times
Walked out the door while still crying
Every time I walk away
Feels like a piece of me is dying
I am weak
He beats me he doesn't complete me
He beats me he doesn't complete me
He beats me he doesn't complete me
And I let him
Please help

Logic

Not hard to understand

Harder to accept

Knowing what you hold in mind

Is exactly what you've kept

All thinking is in the past

Creating present aware

Imprisoned will serving time

Wonder how you got there

Traveling with companion fear

Choke on every illusion

Entrapped mind in logical thought

Sweet bed of delusion's confusion

Discomfort yes, there is an end

Yet, few rarely find

To be released from all fear

Change your mind about your mind

Bad Fruit

Must heal myself

Energy exposed to you

Feeling broken

Signals warning true

Just gotta stop tryin'

To please you

Must reveal myself

Heart where it shouldn't be

Back-tracking on my journey

Just gotta stop tryin'

To make a lie true

Everything everything

Clear from the start

Accepted you and all you're not

Everything you are I already got

Deficient self-love is my plot

Minister of stance dreamer of dreams

Desires affinity of chance among other things

Stuck in fear the easy defense

Looking through eyes of others
Does not equal a glance
Like being alive living in a hearse
Life's blows can feel like a curse
Refusing truth ensures complication
Dreams under burdens—no win situation
Make wise choices keep it clean
Resolve conflict know what accountability means
Between truth and lies and the depth of space
All rotten apple's must be replaced
Holding on to a lie doesn't make it true
Why eat fruit that sickens you?

Serendipity

Stress and strife let's make life

Will you be my earthly wife?

Teach me love and sacrifice

Accept my iniquity

By some chance as we dance

We'll experience serendipity

I need forgiveness everyday

Will blame you when I lose my way

Abuse with words I choose to say

Expect you to love me anyway

Never ever 'splain my state

Believe in fate and won't hesitate

To choose myself over everyone

Beg for the stars forget about the Son

Disrupt peace and serenity

Despise strength of your mentality

Practice faith to my benefit

Stand in the rain complain when wet

Spew self-hatred and speak with regret

Discover I'm not happy yet
When I've had my fill of you
I'll throw you away like an old shoe
Yes, we walked a mile or two
But I've got something else I want to do
Don't hate me I didn't give you the druthers
You over committed to the happiness of others
Give credit to yourself
For what we went through
Magical momments we can't undo
When life's empty and I need something to do
Love of my life I'll come looking for you

Junkie Mind

I'm not in control of your emotionality

O, why O why are you so mad at me?

Perception direction creates reality

O why O why is anger towards me

For I'm not a player

This is not my concern

Your struggle is internal

You're wrestling with the Son

Expert in doing

All things that don't work

Junkie filled mind

But I'm the jerk

What's really going on?

Can't

Can't talk to you when my judgment is on

Too much self-pity around your throne

It's too damn dark in your room

Sadness madness all consumes

And I don't like it

So, I'll choose when we engage

'Cause you're always in a cage

Never want to turn to page

Keep calling it a phase… a stage

Not knowing the illness of rage

Cab Calloway hi-dy, hi-dy, hi-dy, ho

Off the yellow brick road

And to hell with the rainbow

I can't do this anymo'

Choices

You're the fool that's been fooling you
You're the fool that's been fooling you
Creating faking sabotaging too
Creating faking sabotaging too
Why o' why would you do this to you?
Why o' why would you do this to you?
Don't act don't act don't act brand new
You knew what you said yes to
So, really you're mad at you

Petty

You so petty

like a fat man eating spaghetti

While he's sweaty

One noodle at a time

like your mind

One penny to ten-thousand dimes

Aware

Gotta a lotta stuff going on inside

The game of life won't let you hide

Lie to self because of pride

Play denial and judge your trial

Gotta a lotta stuff going on inside

Quitting Time

Always manage to let you down

Am I really much fun to have around?

Saying it's not me... it's you

Let's end this mess and be through

No guilt just release

No grief just peace

I'm not what you like

Can't ride your bike

The seat has spikes

Nothing's in store

We've made life a bore

Breathing fear eats like rust

No trust brings fevers of disgust

Before long we return to dust

Where'd time go? Regret will know

And always show... so, leave

Who This?

Who this?

What's your whim your desire

Liar, liar big fat liar

Inspired, tired, work, play

Land of energy day by day

Passive time killing me

No such thing as sanity

Eating on whatever fed

Know your mind is in my head

Can wonder through in any order

Dark side don't want to bother

Trusted few allowed in space

Like cold water in the face

Trace taste spirit is free

Forgetting sets possibility

Seeing things from all sides

From me I can no longer hide

Rarely do I walk on the ground

Plugged ears annoyed by sound

Of the confused
Let me peruse this vicinity
Who this?
I want to see the remedy
You helped me walk into me
Destroy old tapes called reality
Broke the chains of apathy
Expanded my survivability
Who this?

Bargaining

Bargaining... making a deal with God

Lord if you... I promise... I will...

Trying to hustle the creator

The cremator the regulator

Deep in delusional arrogance

Ego says, there's a chance to bargain

Like dealing with Marvin

And solving a problem

Like robbing time from a clock

Funk from a sock

A hard place from a rock

Stupid I be when focused on me

Not on the purpose of connection

The drip-drop of chemotherapy

Liquid poison never cures infection

She paid the price of hope

Got pumped with chemical dope

We all watched it choke

It took her life

She was my daddy's wife

My sista's mom

Only had one son

Now her life is done

Away we want to run...yeah

So, I try to bargain

Like I'm dealing with Marvin

All the while starving

For God

Missing You

I can't think of you and not cry

even though I know the reasons why

It doesn't make it any easier

This reality I can't escape

Intensity of grief I cannot take

Here there everywhere

More than I care

Something I can't share

'Cause it's so personal

I can't give it away

Like your voice

or making a choice

You own it

It owns you

Some days some days

You make it through

Other days you find you

Watching you

Do the best impression of living

Without confession of the pain stain

Life simply remains changed

Forever

It doesn't get better

It ages with time

The full intention only reminds

me of what's missing

I can't think of you and not cry

Although I know the reasons why

...just missing you

Good Grief

I cannot measure grief

or pain behind your eyes

I only know the ground I've walked

and the sound of sweet goodbyes

I wonder if I couldn't feel

would I be here this day?

Or, would I just pass you by

and stare when you say

I just miss her, her I just miss

Personal

Loss is so damn personal

You must experience to understand

Like listening without ears

A mind filled with sand

Un-transferable personal

Some take longer to know

Breathe, pause, pray, let go

With or without you, life goes on

Words cannot articulate the pain of wrong

Nothing's the same but all remains

Look at the world everything's changed

Old eyes see a new view of mortality

Every name on the list—next could be me

For a period of seasons, you'll mourn loss

Time doesn't heal it only exhaust —the mind

Draining the eye of every tear

Whispers of sadness fill the ear

A flood of emotion can't define devotion

The adoration of its kind

Personal and un-transferable

Loss is more than mine

Enveloping, developing, engulfing no doubt

How I should be? I got to get this out

Incomparable for sure no two are the same

Un-transferable and personal qualities remain

Sin of mistake you can't correct

Don't understand

The Lord ain't through yet

Forced to accept what has taken place

Looking for peace through mercy and grace

Personally painful it can only be

Who understands mortality?

Too Much Sauce

No one can do anything about me being gone

Where you feel you are is a place called alone

In frustration

A season of self destruction is a personal situation

So, you will not understand my plan

to get as high as I can

The pain of living—pressures every man

White, black, brown, my brother

Sister, aunt, cousin, son, dad, mother

I miss you

Hell can get attention but don't listen

Seek the spirit of the One and conquer quick

Listen to the Word don't believe in sh**

Don't get too much sauce you'll get lost in it

Heavy, heavy, heavy emotional day

Nothing stops my fears from flowing my way

These walls are solid my mind is crazy

Caught battling demons I'm just blazing

I know there were times when I gave you a fit

Truth be told I wasn't easy to deal with

The pain of mental anguish is a real thing

I could feel my phantom it wasn't just in my brain

Don't judge my walk for madness you've done it too

I believed in the master I did make it through

Too much sauce a misstep a mistake

We must face our fear in order to escape

The pain of grief is hard to release

I want you to know I found my peace

I'm safe in his arms not deceased

Looking over your shoulder I am free

How many red birds do you have to see?

I Emot

Emotions for the present

Some I've known

Emotions from the past

I've fully grown

A beginning is an ending

Life's lived and gone

Engulfed with loss

The inside of alone

Outside illusions remain the same

Experience of truth...forever changed

Immersed mind hears the sound

Language of those no longer around

Emotions for the present

Some I have known

Emotions from the past are full grown

I miss you

Blame

Didn't say it was your fault.

Just said I blame you

I used to give a shit.

But now I take pills for that.

ISNESS

"Isness" is where I am. I've come here to be me.

Isness

Isness isn't what you think

Isness is what makes your eyes blink

Isness isn't the story you've been told

Isness is the intelligence a molecule holds

Isness isn't what the physical eye see

Isness is where I've come to be

Isness is you

Isness is me

My Day

Started with low energy

A poor attitude and a flat tire

And it wasn't even Monday

Drank a Red Bull with bacon and eggs

Put on headphones to drown my dread

Coffee

Nothing is alright

But everything is okay

This little lie helps me

Make it through the day

Composition

Mind rich

Heart heavy

Ground gray

Are you ready?

Time limited

Do you believe in time?

Universe can speak

Believe it's mine

People stuck in I don't know

I am energy I must flow

Indecision

What 'am gone do with this fire inside?

Cain't keep it, Lawd, i cain't keep it

What' am gone do with all this pride?

Cain't swallow it, i jus' cain't

If i could show—they would see

What if they don't like the truest me?

So close, so close, oh so near

Cain't do nothing with all this fear

What'am gone do with all this fire?

This fire, Lawd this fire

Dirty

I must play in the dirt

This is the grind

I am a practitioner

My life is my mind

Complaining is useless

Get out of your rut

This is the grind

Play in the dirt

The land is fruitful

Waiting for me to possess

Inside my heart where dreams rest

Get up! Do something!

You got one life

Get through the noise

Create paradise

Get dirty

U stop U

Always saying what you gonna do

Look in the mirror only you stop you

Work with the hard answer

The one you don't want to hear

Love takes labor stop nursing fear

Lazy—your go to

Sluggish your best friend

Plans lie inside

Too pathetic to begin

There is no hidden power

No need to dig down deep

When things get tough

You reward yourself with sleep

Internal roadblocks you create

Indifference towards life you cannot fake

Begin to manage what's on your plate

Become the hero instead of arch-enemy

Stop wasting life claim your victory

Matchup

Do your actions match your energy?
What your thoughts really think
Do your thoughts match your energy?
Is your mind in sync?
Are you aligned with "who"
you've asked to be?
Are you still making excuses?
living in fantasy
Are you fantasy famous?
A legend in your mind
Skipping steps exalting self
Not listening to the Divine
Use people as props
Give with a closed hand
Angry with God
'Cause this isn't what you planned
Seeking to uplift yourself
Forgetting lives are interwoven
Only one true path exist

Not the one you've chosen

Detour is not "by accident"

Open your ears so you can see

If you want a leg-up

Match spirit's energy

Interview

Do you have any openings?

I like to go deep

Into the peace of piece

Where there's no need for sleep

Job surface is the middle

Build slowly, destroy swiftly

Know the riddle or get played like a fiddle

Programmed behavior where problems lie

Impulsive gratification makes the insatiable cry

Power plays of importance where ego lives

When needs aren't met whims aren't fulfilled

Job is the place

Where the self-absorbed debate

Grumble, cuss, deteriorate

Choose what's not wanted and call it fate

This is not the place for me

I'm looking for fullness of possibility

Limitlessness...what makes you me

Inside of humanness—oneness of "One"

The road that walks a path to the Son

Emotions run like water ending truth and time

Reap the harvest of labor ascension of mind

Seek levels, lives, naked grace

No contract called time no place called space

Veil of separation never worn

No dominate will, no pressure to perform

No past, present, future...no thing called history

The place where reason has no authority

Seed and feed til' dead and gone

Rule out thought and sit on the throne

That's the job I want

Do you have something in that department?

Let Go

You know this road and how it ends

Must let go to begin again

What you know is obsolete

You know why you can't sleep

Rise, rise to a higher dimension

Look for the edge of ascension

Throwing fits waste the day

Awake or asleep things don't go your way

There is only one way why question it?

To what you apply rejection fits

Practice understanding detachment

Don't chase the feeling of being right

Manage emotions or lose daylight

Judge the world man is most deceiving

Just like you he has reason

Storing misery recalling pain

Destructive cycles warn the sane

You know this road and how it ends

Let go and don't come back here again

Go just Go!

Go over to the sink

Please pour me a drink

I'm trying to think

About something

Go outside

Please take a ride

I'm trying to hear

What's near

Go away

Just do you

I'm trying to see

Me without you

Me Time

I spend an awful lot of time wit' myself

Do I really need to know me that well?

Spend an awful lotta time with myself

So much I told me to go to hell

Shoved me around, cussed me out too

Apologized to myself for putting me thru

All that hell

Like I said... I spend an awful lotta time with myself

Wrote me a letter to break up with me

Put it in the mail so I could see

Who in the hell was writing me?

Read the letter, broke my heart

Called me up and prayed to God—that I'd answer

I needed to see why I wanted to stop seeing me

Got no answer hung up the phone

Looked self in the mirror

And said, leave me alone

This began an argument

Between the person in the mirror

And who I spent time with
Back and forth the shout was on
I was determined to leave me alone
Finally, a hush fell over the room
Energy of silence began to consume
Communication
Fighting with oneself
A no-win situation
Observation and self-examination
Self-destruction and de-appreciation
Constructed bonds of limitation
Standing for rights and righting wrongs
Concocting wisdom all homegrown
A fool using the comparison tool
Tryin reshape self on the potter's stool
Need a healing—o Bethesda pool
Do you want to get well?"
Out of control there is no sound
Lowered head dropped to the ground
Submission

Introspection... the fluid of correction

A spiritual transfusion released confusion

Exaggerated importance of who I be

Path to learning a personal journey

Heard what I had to forget

Remembered what I needed to see

Did what I could not understood

Read a book opened in me

Every word a planted seed

Reconnected sovereignty

Every day is better

I can't wait to spend time with me

Super Hero

When it comes to desire

Is your soul on fire?

Does faith reach higher?

Are you the liar?

Where are you when you need you?

When your mind won't stop talking too?

When you want to be quiet

Mind continues to chatter

Step into your greater self

Exactly what is the matter?

Place your mind under attention

Don't let it interfere

Become your super hero

Push pass pain and fear

If you want to change your life

You must save yourself

Recognize the place

It's exactly where you left.

Hush!

You run your mouth so much

You bypass truth

Been a big mouth

Early patterns since youth

Pride queen of remedial stuff

Chasing "being right" isn't enough

Pointing out infractions

Always seeking to win

Ruining connections

Wonder why you don't have friends

Big fish in a small pond

Think you're ahead of the pack

Take a look over your shoulder

No one has your back

Privilege you've messed up

Arrogance fills your mouth up

A fool is unsure

Everyone knows you're insecure

Waste brainwaves looking for control

Migraine and stress is where your truth unfolds

Ebb is low you cannot navigate

Highly charged emotions you cannot escape

Pushing your own buttons

Knowing answers without seeking

Practice walking in truth before you start speaking

Hush!

Blockhead

Ego blocked my joy today
What do I have to say
Ego blocked my joy today
It really happened this way
Bitching and moaning filled my space
Wore a mean pouty face
Bent any ear didn't acknowledge grace
Listen to ego—mind split
Ricochet conversations create a fit
Inner conflict familiar ground
Power of spirit are you around?
Illusion of rejection lack of self love
Feeling forgotten by the one above
Self-delusion can't rationalize
Enter the pit entertain the lies
Wasted energy taunt with despair
Feeling attacked and nothing's there
I lack nothing I repeat
Where you sit is your belief

Moved

Somewhere in-between

Crying and fear

What the hell is this?

I need you here

Near

Learning to live

Without love one's

Consequence of becoming

Chasing dreams...creating things

Puts you somewhere in-between

Crying and fear

Values built on material gain

Devoid of passion family brings

Staying connected is key

Create what's missing

A new reality

Oneness and being-ness

The perils of choice

Don't compromise principle or lose voice

Selection plays a major part

Expressing who you are is pure ART

Stay tuned to presence of you and me

Or create a lifetime of agony

God and family let nothing divide

Everything else steeped in pride

Stay connected never are you alone

God and family is always home

LOL

You so phony

Can't even call you baloney

Like powered cheese on macaroni

But you think you Big Homey

Like an elephant thinking he's a pony

You got it way wrong

This has gone on for far too long

Your three-legged stool is not a throne

Someone else's house is not your home

Arrived you have not

Telling lies is not a plot

But you can believe anything

When you build life off virtual themes

and stuff you've read...no credentials

did I forget to mention?

you're a phony, fraud, fake mistake

your result is the same

because you can't communicate

Other Side

A woman knows...if she's gonna

Do you, screw you, be good 2 you

Without any input from you

She knows...how she's gonna

Show you, teach you, learn you, reach you

Without your two-cent

So, don't get hell bent

On your version of common sense

Because a woman ain't common

She's a flowing stream

Of ocean dreams

A place you can only visualize

Being part of her scene

She knows what she wants

And how to get it too

Your job is to do what she asks you to

Just like you did with yo' mama

Don't test her patience

For it leads to drama

You've got to learn to

Listen with your eyes

See with your ears

Speak with your touch

Breathe in her tears

Smell her emotions and when they rise

Take them and make them interpret your sighs

...of relief and release peace

God is at her right and love is her light

She's content not because of common sense

because she knows what she is and isn't too

Without any input coming from you

Hang Up!

Please understand

You don't have to hold the phone

If it's your desire

Simply say, "leave me alone"

I don't call you to talk to myself

So...you don't have anything to say?

A simple what's going on or, how was your day

...would suffice

However, this is a day when nothing's nice

Again, our love pays the price

For poor choices made in life

Stubbornness is really not a crime

It's the rudimentary lie

Pretending everything is fine

Don't waste time holding the line

Hang up

Self-Trap

Sad but true

You play the fool with you

The lie you love just ain't true

Some things you just want to do

Trapping yourself

Boxing "you" in

Patterns and themes

You fully understand

No shift in awareness

No need to compare

Imposed will upon self

Will keep you there

Exactly where you want to be

Self-manipulation

Creates the chaos you see

Selfish

Who's needs come first?

Recognize the one-sided curse

We never discussed rehearsed

How imbalanced happiness would feel

Without the thrill of connection

A blocked view doesn't change passion

I still love you

Can only control what I do or say

So, love me, love me anyway

Anyhow, today, right now

Eventually we'll get to you somehow

I put my needs first

I'm selfish

Warnings

Your vibrations are strong

It's easy for you to do wrong

Your vibrations are strong

Too easy for you to do wrong

Better leave you alone

Energy does not lie

A time bomb ticks

A hazard to yourself

You jokingly admit

Demons running around

Witnesses to truth

Pain of being left

Lingers like a bad tooth

Engage rage power unknown

Nothing strikes without a warning

Better leave you alone

Self Seduction

Seduced myself into thinking

You wanted me

Something about me, something in me

You don't, didn't, never have

You desired, admired, was tired

Wanted a refreshment

But never imagined

How time would be spent

What it would mean

Being a part of my daily scene

That was me not you

Let's be true

Your most important factor

Will always be you

Never thought how the ear

Would love to hear

Special words drip off the right lips

Drink every drop sip, sip

Sink or, swim it's all false true

This situation wreaks of dodo

Turning over thoughts

Can't live without you

Not letting you off the hook

'Cause there is none

Empty shame game called having fun

Someone's left holding the love gun

Escapade from domesticated life

Boredom with your lovely wife

Stages of cheating changes the hue

Fragrance of my flower belongs to you

Seduction laced fantasy

Maybe just, maybe you and me

Could be something...

Some "thing" we are

Indescribable, unreliable, undeniable

Untrue thing

You wanted attention I wanted a ring

Weakened vows produce stain

Lust entered minds our world is not the same

Ignited temptation filled your time
Levels of sensory thoughts of free mind
Luxury of hidden adultery
Practiced artisan stop playing with me
Mind's eye see the knife
Go back go back to your lovely wife
Sinfully you play king of the thrown
Before I hurt you boy, gone on

Sometimes II

Sometimes poetry is so dark

As dark as me

The power source I can't see

Fights with internal wit

Can cause unintended fits

Daily report from the dark

Crying loudly is this art?

Alone is crazy

Homeless people amazing

A permanent look "save me"

Disconnected mind filled with funk of senses

Whose stupid idea was picket fences?

Water ain't free, earth ain't property

Man's game called captivity

Played every day in the land of free

Oh, My Country tis' of Thee

Spoke not of tyranny

For justice cannot be for all

Or, thou caste system would certainly fall

Sometimes poetry is so dark

As dark as me

Darkness is the strength of me

Changed

Something happened to me today

Spiritual not lyrical kind of way

Uncontrollably under control

Ever happen to you?

When you know energy is flowing through

Doesn't require permission from you

Like, you can't stop crying until crying stops

Or dying until dying stops

Or, laughing until laughing stops

Or, hurting until hurting stops

Pivotal moments will lead you home

Exit virtual reality where we all roam

Fleeting II

You caused me to write

Damn near every night

But that's cool

Better than being your fool

Thought

Thought is energy

My thoughts rest on you

Causing an effect

Have I stumbled upon true...love?

Yum Yum

Black orchid orange mango

Butter nut honey suckle

You bring light to my life

I think of you and chuckle

Nectar of my natural

Kink in my hair

Pooch in my pouch

Let me breathe your air

Flavor of sweetness

Flash back to August heat

Laying eyes on you—an instant treat

Yum yum give me you

What wasn't there is now true

Like atoms and air cover my moon

I'm waiting for you please return soon

First Thing

I woke with you in mind

Hope I wasn't alone in that span of time

Didn't seem to be energetically

Hmmm...how do you do that to me

Enter my space

Without a single trace of evidence

Our time so short spent

If only one day it was still meant

To be

Something about you

Colors my gray sky blue

And, I like it

The grin on my face

The something in my eyes

I only want you to see

Heart cannot speak of lies

And, I like it

Grin in on my face

Something in my eyes

Only want you to see
Heart can't speak of lies
Think of you
Metabolism rises
Thoughts rest on you
Have I stumbled upon true?

Sweet Spot

Discovered I could love

Allowed myself to

Felt amazing blazing

Filled my hope

Just like that

Love was made visible

And then I woke

Hmmm...I was so into you

IDK

What we gonna be?

'Cause I can't pretend

Are we gonna be

More than friends?

Walls

So full of pain

Can't experience pleasure

Internal war

There is no measure

Walls the walls

Can't break through

But so badly wants to love you

What's a girl to do?

Walls of pain restrict the view

Cross her path she's searching for true

And wants to love you kinsman

Mistakes

All mistakes are errors of ignorance

No one... everyone's a robot

I don't know what I forgot

But you do

Holding it like ransom

However handsome

I can't love a portion of you

I must include this funk too

For certain I don't wanna

Cannot control what you gonna

Position I seek is to forgive

Perceived offense so I can live

Things appear different from a certain angle

Why choose to mangle and dangle our love?

Facts and acts stated as truth

Interpretation of life no excuse

I know what I did and so do you

Holding on is blackmail igniting personal hell

Punished love the evidence of negligence

You'll never understand what doesn't make sense

Apology and penance a quick remedy

Squelches the tip of insecurity

Every day is the best opportunity

Push pass the haze of misery

Not a forgetting a letting go

Why let a mistake steal the show?

Mistakes absorb hours of attention

Did I mention...

I don't know what I hurt

But you do

Forgive me love my sorry is true

Life is too short

Truth Juice

I like the way you look on me

God, I do

See you in my eyes

Wanna talk to you

Feel you in my breath

Oxygen to my cells

Where this ride goes

Only time will tell

I'm not scared

Tickled no doubt

Tingling and buzzing

Makes me wanna shout

I really like the way you look on me

Too bad it isn't love

Just fantasy

Speak-easy

I speak my truth

Don't care who understand

I'm in love

Are you lust's villain?

Speak easy

It's just you and me

Write words on my heart

Call it poetry

Kinsman

Of you I dreamt last night
Albeit not a hair contrite
Our spirits exchanged delight
Kinsman of you I dreamt last night

Read Me

I like it when you read me

Changing state of reality

Silence my conscious with presence

Peel layers show my best

Something about your energy

Connects me to joy and rest

Can ease into anything with you

Laughing and watching as I do

Falling left, right, center view

I can hear your silence too

Read me morning, noon and night

Delicious is the taste of every bite

Proposals

If I stay when I come

What will you say when it's done?

What if you like it as much as I do?

Will you look at me through new eyes?

Or, hide the truth behind sin's carnal lies

Headed for trouble

No, it's just a thought

Hesitation an annoying state

For not doing what you ought

You've thought about it a billion times

All of the dreams turn out fine

So, when I stay what will we play...

Blackberry Kisses

I got blackberry kisses for you

Wanting you to be in

See me from a different position

What I got won't fit

Can't start what I quit

So, I'm bothered

You got that thang I need

Sampled through chemistry

In my dream come to me

Over and over

Made room for you

You're somethin' to do

Thought I'd never find

Emotionally walking the line

Is this infidelity?

Never confirmed physically

Because of virtue

I run to you

Blackberry kisses I have for you

Ummm

Even though you're not here

I bite my lips tracing the taste of your flavor

I miss you

In its fullness, flavor enhances my vigor

For something called "life"

I need you

Your effect causes my disorder

Divert my path

Invade my privacy

Provoke my thinking

Ummm... I like that

Ummm 2

You make me think about things

Love...loving...slow dancing

Laughing...playing...hips swaying

Moist is voice

Quiet daydreaming smiling wanting

Curious

I wonder what love is like

No Benies

My mature mind loved you

You just couldn't see

Because of immaturity

How we could be

Now you miss me

Replay me like a vinyl

Vintage wreckage of desire

Chained burden love

Doesn't create fire

My mature mind loved you

aRt

Thoughts of you

On pages of heart

Why are we apart

When we're each other's aRt

Just Saying

Since you're not going to

take care of me any better

than currently

I've decided

I won't be giving you

my currency

Thank You

Shattered splattered fantasy

You walked out

No idea how to cope

Pain of loving you

Tightened my neck like a rope

I got to know me

How I think, value, enjoy, hate

Called our experience a sorry mistake

It wasn't

Energy bonded created chemistry

Naturally attracted you were to me

Infusion of negative mentally

Our chained reaction changed satisfaction

Learned new meaning—addition, subtraction

Complication, hesitation, self-centeredness

Revealed what needed to be addressed

Pain of loving you opened the door

I needed to love you less and love me more

Rejection betrayal shattered fantasy

Pain of loving you helped me find me

Thank you

Do

Do the thing you don't want to do

That's the only way to deal with you

Take the hardest road first

Learn the terrain

From there you'll be able

To measure your gain

Be relentless in the pursuit of life

Face head on turmoil and strife

Once you realize it's up to you

You'll see you're the thing

You don't want to do

About the Author

De'Broada, is a featured spoken word poet at community events throughout Kansas. She performs spoken word poetry to form connections between the audience and the madness experienced in life. Her use of word play, voice inflection and other stylistic elements leaves a poem open to multiple interpretations. Her oral art exposes many conditions and the deep work of becoming self-aware and help many identify with the struggle our strong, stubborn, rebellious personalities can create, thus, turning our worlds upside down. She believes, words are vehicles of power that can inspire action and healing. In her words, "The way I see it, life is training...to become me. And, if you can't be honest with yourself when no one is watching, you're in a world of trouble."

She is also the author of My Way: Finding My Way Back to Me (iCreativ Books 2017).

Follow her on Facebook @ iCreativProperti or,
http://www.icreativproperti.com/

www.ingramcontent.com/pod-product-compliance
Lightning Source LLC
LaVergne TN
LVHW091302080426
835510LV00007B/356